creating professional drum loops

by Ed Roscetti

Amsco Publications
A Part of **The Music Sales Group**
New York/London/Paris/Sydney/Copenhagen/Berlin/Tokyo/Madrid

Project Editor: Felipe Orozco
Graphic Design: Sol & Luna Creations

For Loop Licensing and usage fees contact Roscetti Music
at www.roscettimusic.com or call 818-508-5882.

Order No. AM 978615
US International Standard Book Number: 0.8256.2836.9
UK International Standard Book Number:1.84449.242.7

Exclusive Distributors:
Music Sales Corporation
257 Park Avenue South, New York, NY. 10010 USA

Music Sales Limited
8/9 Frith Street, London W1D 3JB England

Music Sales Pty. Limited
120 Rothschild Street, Rosebery, Sydney, NSW 2018, Australia

Printed in the United States of America
by Vicks Lithograph and Printing Corporation

Table of Contents

CD Tracks

1. **Olodum** – Full Mix   ♩=96
2. **Olodum** – Drumset Only
3. **Olodum** – Percussion Only
4. **Olodum** – Quick Load Full Mix 4a

   Olodum – Quick Load Drumset Only 4b

   Olodum – Quick Load Percussion Only 4c
5. **Funk/Hip–Hop** – Full Mix   ♩=108
6. **Funk/Hip–Hop** – Drumset Only
7. **Funk/Hip–Hop** – Percussion Only
8. **Funk/Hip–Hop** – Quick Load Full mix 8a

   Funk/Hip–Hop – Quick Load Drumset Only 8b

   Funk/Hip–Hop – Quick Load Percussion Only 8c
9. **Tom–Tom Groove** – Full Mix   ♩=106
10. **Tom–Tom Groove** – Drumset Only
11. **Tom–Tom Groove** – Percussion Only
12. **Tom–Tom Groove** – Quick Load Full Mix 12a

    Tom–Tom Groove – Quick Load Drumset Only 12b

    Tom–Tom Groove – Quick Load Percussion only 12c
13. **Hip–Hop 1** – Full Mix   ♩=115
14. **Hip–Hop 1** – Drumset only
15. **Hip–Hop 1** – Percussion Only
16. **Hip–Hop 1** – Quick Load Full Mix 16a

    Hip–Hop 1 – Quick Load Drumset Only 16b

    Hip–Hop 1 – Quick Load Percussion Only 16c
17. **Hip–Hop 2** – Full mix   ♩=88
18. **Hip–Hop 2** – Drumset only
19. **Hip–Hop 2** – Percussion Only
20. **Hip–Hop 2** – Quick Load Full Mix 20a

    Hip–Hop 2 – Quick Load Drumset Only 20b

    Hip–Hop 2 – Quick Load Percussion Only 20c
21. **Hip–Hop 3** (programmed) – Full Mix   ♩=86

22. **Hip–Hop 3** (programmed) – Drumset only
23. **Hip–Hop 3** (programmed) – Percussion Only
24. **Hip–Hop 3** (programmed) – Quick Load Full Mix 24a

    Hip–Hop 3 (programmed) – Quick Load Drumset Only 24b

    Hip–Hop 3 (programmed) – Quick Load Percussion Only 24c
25. **Hip–Hop 4** (programmed) – Full Mix   ♩=120
26. **Hip–Hop 4** (programmed) – Quick Load Full Mix
27. **Funk March** – Full Mix   ♩=85
28. **Funk March** – Quick Load Drumset Only
29. **Drum Cadence** – Full Mix   ♩=96
30. **Drum Cadence** – Quick Load Drumset Only
31. **Funk 1** – Full Mix   ♩=90
32. **Funk 1** – Drumset only
33. **Funk 1** – Percussion Only
34. **Funk 1** – Quick Load Full Mix 34a

    Funk 1 – Quick Load Drumset Only 34b

    Funk 1 – Quick Load Percussion Only 34c
35. **Funk 2** – Full Mix   ♩=104
36. **Funk/Rock 3** – Full Mix   ♩=124
37. **Funk/Rock 3** – Quick Load Full Mix
38. **Funk 4** – Full Mix   ♩=133
39. **Funk 4** – Quick Load Full Mix
40. **Straight-Eighth Rock** – Full Mix   ♩=120
41. **Straight-Eighth Rock** – Drumset Only
42. **Straight-Eighth Rock** – Percussion Only
43. **Straight-Eighth Rock** – Quick Load Full Mix 43a

    Straight-Eighth Rock – Quick Load Drumset Only 43b

    Straight-Eighth Rock – Quick Load Percussion Only 43c
44. **Rock Shuffle** – Full Mix   ♩=130
45. **Rock Shuffle** – Quick Load Full Mix
46. **Rock Blues** $^{12}_{8}$ – Full Mix   ♩=116

CD Tracks

47. **Rock Blues** 12/8 – Quick Load Full Mix

48. **Slow Blues** 12/8 – Full Mix ♩=126

49. **Slow Blues** 12/8 – Quick Load Full Mix

50. **Africa 1** – Full Mix ♩=64

51. **Africa 1** – Drumset only

52. **Africa 1** – Percussion Only

53. **Africa 1** – Quick Load Full Mix 53a

    Africa 1 – Quick Load Drumset Only 53b

    Africa 1 – Quick Load Percussion Only 53c

54. **Africa 2** – Full Mix ♩=55

55. **Africa 2** – Drumset only

56. **Africa 2** – Percussion Only

57. **Africa 2** – Quick Load Full Mix 57a

    Africa 2 – Quick Load Drumset Only 57b

    Africa 2 – Quick Load Percussion Only 57c

58. **Africa 3** – Full Mix ♩=104

59. **Africa 3** – Drumset only

60. **Africa 3** – Percussion Only

61. **Africa 3** – Quick Load Full Mix 61a

    Africa 3 – Quick Load Drumset Only 61b

    Africa 3 – Quick Load Percussion Only 61c

62. **Samba 1** – Full Mix ♩=104

63. **Samba 1** – Drumset only

64. **Samba 1** – Percussion Only

65. **Samba 1** – Quick Load Full Mix 65a

    Samba 1 – Quick Load Drumset Only 65b

    Samba 1 – Quick Load Percussion Only 65c

66. **Samba March** – Full Mix ♩=84

67. **Samba March** – Drumset only

68. **Samba March** – Percussion Only

69. **Samba March** – Quick Load Full Mix 69a

    Samba March – Quick Load Drumset Only 69b

    Samba March – Quick Load Percussion Only 69c

70. **Samba** 2/4 – Full Mix ♩=102

71. **Samba** 2/4 – Drumset only

72. **Samba** 2/4 – Percussion Only

73. **Samba** 2/4 – Quick Load Full Mix 73a

    Samba 2/4 – Quick Load Drumset Only 73b

    Samba 2/4 – Quick Load Percussion Only 73c

74. **Funk Olodum** – Full Mix ♩=91.92

75. **Funk Olodum** – Quick Load Full Mix

76. **Rock Olodum** – Full Mix ♩=104

77. **Rock Olodum** – Quick Load Full Mix

78. **Funk 5** – Full Mix ♩=100

79. **Funk 5** – Quick Load Full Mix

80. **Funk Swing** – Full Mix ♩=100

81. **Funk Swing** – Quick Load Full Mix

82. **Rock 1** – Full Mix ♩=79

83. **Rock 1** – Quick Load Full Mix

84. **Hip–Hop 5** – Full Mix ♩=126

85. **Hip–Hop 5** – Quick Load Full Mix

86. **Straight-Eighth Rock 2** – Full Mix ♩=87

87. **Straight-Eighth Rock 2** – Quick Load Full Mix

88. **Sixteenth–Note Rock with Toms** – Full Mix ♩=96

89. **Sixteenth–Note Rock with Toms** – Quick Load Full Mix

90. **Rock** 6/8 – Full Mix ♩.=94

91. **Rock** 6/8 – Quick Load Full Mix

92. **Funk Rock** 2/4 – Full Mix ♩=120

93. **Funk Rock** 2/4 – Quick Load Full Mix

Foreword

Ed finally makes it easy to understand how to create drum and percussion loops. Everything is laid out perfectly in the text, with detailed descriptions of instruments played, head combinations, sticks used, and notations of all his *Quick Load* loops. The CD is set up to import stereo audio loops into any digital realm, with a variety of drumset and percussion loops, drumset only loops, and percussion only loops. Ed's loop concepts are a must for drummers, programmers, composers, and all musicians.

Joe Porcaro

About the Book and CD

The Drum Loop Reference Guide in chapter one will get you to any loop quickly in the text and on the CD. Also, each loop in every chapter is self-contained (if you want to jump around the book and CD).

Note: Because there are specific topics of discussion at the beginning of some chapters, I would suggest starting from the beginning of a chapter if you are going to go out of order.

Important: Check out how to use the loops in Chapter Two before you start importing loops off the audio CD.

This book/CD package is for drummers, programmers, composers, and all musicians.

Introduction

Some of my favorite drum and percussion takes in the studio are ones that are real-time, beginning-to-end takes. They have that first-time energy that you sometimes just can't get again. That's why I always say the first take (or the run-through) is usually the best, and that's why we always keep *Pro Tools* in "record" at my studio.

All the loops were recorded in two 8-hour sessions and most are first and second takes. There are no *Pro Tools* time edits or fixes on these loops. I wanted to capture a real-time moment with the grooves for the CD. I overdubbed to the programmed beats using the same concept. The drumset only, percussion only, and all the Quick Load loops were edited out of the longer performance loops. Have fun with creating your own loops or editing and using the loops on the audio CD.

Chapter 1 • Drum loop concepts & loop reference guide

The way drummers work these days has changed drastically from the pre-MIDI days. Let's look back for a moment and appreciate the changes. Before 1981, every drum track was recorded with a live drummer. Recording with a live rhythm section (drums, bass, guitars, and piano) was the way to track at recording sessions. Then the *Linn Drum LM1* and *Linn Drum 2* came out and changed everything.

Drum machine-driven tracks became the norm during the eighties. Everyone was programming beats for records, films, television, and jingles. It became the new sound that everyone wanted. It also made anyone with good rhythmic ideas a drummer and/or percussionist. In the nineties, the alternative rock scene hit and the sounds of live rhythm sections were back, while rap and hip-hop started to explode with programmed drumbeats and drum loops.

So here we are in 2004 and drum loops are bigger than ever. Let's get started using some simple ways to create a library of your own drum and percussion loops.

The next time you're in a studio recording with your band or doing a session for someone, make sure to have a blank digital audio tape with you. Almost all studios still have DAT machines, and it is very easy for the engineer to bus you over to the DAT and record your drum sounds and beats. If he records your drum sounds into *Pro Tools*, then he has to burn you a CD, and that takes time. This way, you make it easy on him by using the DAT tape. You can then transfer your performance later to any digital audio workstation. Ask the engineer if he would record you while he is getting drum sounds. After you do all the individual hits on the drums, cymbals, *etc.* (which will be very useful to you if you own a sampler), it will be time to play the whole kit. At this time you should be prepared to play grooves at the tempos you want, which you can later load into the DAW of your choice. This will get you started recording loops of your own. If you don't have your own studio, you can get together with someone later who can edit the loops for you and burn them onto a CD. You will now have a library of loops that you can use when you work for songwriters, producers, and for your own compositions.

Make sure you keep good records of your loops. Notate tempo, style, and time feel. Mix the drum set-ups. Use different sizes for different styles. For example: You might have some rock loops played with larger-sized drums, 22" or 24" bass drums, 13", 14", or 16" toms, and larger cymbals; some funk and hip-hop grooves with a 20" bass drum, 10", 12", and 14" toms; or a jazz kit with an 18" bass drum and 12" and 14" toms. Make a point to mix and match sets. Also, use different sized snare drums and cymbals.

In this book I will notate the drum sizes, cymbals, heads, and percussion for each loop and notate the groove played as well. This will help you get started creating your own drum and percussion loops. Let's talk about the recording equipment and microphones used to record the loops on the CD. Here is a list of microphones and preamps that were used on the CD. Experiment with different microphones and preamps, as well as different mic placements. Remember to use your ears and to document combinations that work, feel, and sound good.

Microphone and Preamp List
Microphones:

Bass Drum 1 (Shure SM91)
The microphone was laid flat on top of the pillow inside the bass drum, which was recorded to a separate track in *Pro Tools*.

Bass Drum 2 – Shure Beta52
The microphone was on a stand just outside the front hole of the bass drum and was recorded to a separate track in *Pro Tools*. This approach enables you to use either bass drum mic in the mix, or combine both mics to come up with your own bass-drum sound.

Snare – Shure SM57
Experiment with this microphone position until you like what you hear. Point the mic away from the hi-hat.

Hi-Hat – Shure SM81
Point the hi-hat microphone away from the snare drum.

Tom-Toms – Shure SM98 Beta
These are clip-on microphones and should be positioned towards the center of the toms.

Popcorn Snare – Shure SM57
Point the microphone away from the hi-hat.

Overhead L and R – Shure KSM32
Experiment with different heights and angles.

Percussion – Soundelux E-47
Overdubs

Mono Room Microphone on Drumset – Soundelux E-47
Use this track to mix in some room sound when you feel its appropriate.

Preamp List:
The *PreSonus DigiMAX* was used on these eight channels recorded optically into *Pro Tools* at a sampling rate of 44.1 kHz.

1. Bass Drum 1
2. Bass Drum 2
3. Snare
4. Hi-hat
5. Tom 1
6. Tom 2
7. Tom 3
8. Popcorn Snare

The *Great River MP2MV* (stereo) mic preamp was used for the drum overheads. Overhead channels went into the *Avalon 2055 EQ*, through the *Apogee Rosetta AD-80* converters, and directly into *Pro Tools*.

Use effects sparingly. If you have a stereo audio loop, you don't want to use too much reverb on the drums. Reverb creates space and if it is recorded on your loops, you can't remove it if it's a stereo loop. I used very little reverb on the CD for that reason. The reverbs used were from the Korg *OASYS* PCI audio card and the Digidesign *RealVerb*. I did not use any external analog reverbs on this project. All reverbs were in the digital domain. Be sure to mix things up by doing some completely dry loops (*i.e.*, no reverb), and then experimenting with your effects to come up with new sounds.

The *drum loop reference guide* located on page four will help you jump around and find different stylized loops on the CD quickly. The *loop reference* charts in each chapter will keep each chapter self-contained.

Chapter 2 • The drumset as an overdub instrument

In this chapter, I will discuss drum overdub concepts. Step back and look at a five-piece drumset. *What do you see?* A bass drum, three tom-toms, a snare drum, hi-hat, ride cymbal, and two crash cymbals. Start off by moving the snare drum, tom-toms, cymbals, and hi-hat out of the way. You are now left with just the bass drum. Put a song on that you like to play along with (in ¼ time) and just play quarter notes on the bass drum all the way through. When you want to break it down, play half notes or whole notes. Move your arms like you are playing hi-hat and snare to help you get in the groove. Feel free to move and dance on the pedal. Every drummer has his or her dance—find your dance. The dance is how your body moves when you are moving your time-feel in the groove. When you finish working on the bass drum, add the snare drum and repeat the process. Remember this time to play the snare drum only (no bass drum). Repeat this process with the hi-hat, ride cymbal, crash cymbals, and tom-toms. This will help you think of each piece of the drumset individually.

Why do we need to do this? Today's drum tracks are sometimes a combination of programmed beats (using samples), loops, and real-time overdubs (real instruments).

Example: You might have to overdub tom fills to a drum loop or add real hi-hat or ride cymbal. I once had to do a snare drum overdub to a programmed loop using brushes. I have also overdubbed bass drum only, played tom fills, or played just hi-hat in the studio. The possibilities are endless.

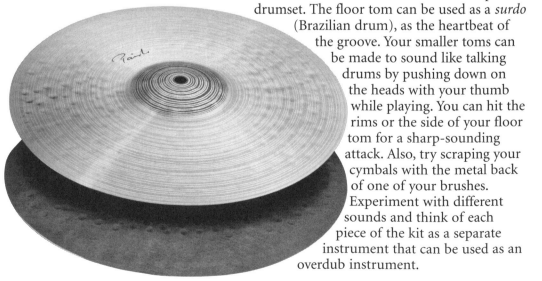

You can make all kinds of sounds with a basic five-piece drumset. The floor tom can be used as a *surdo* (Brazilian drum), as the heartbeat of the groove. Your smaller toms can be made to sound like talking drums by pushing down on the heads with your thumb while playing. You can hit the rims or the side of your floor tom for a sharp-sounding attack. Also, try scraping your cymbals with the metal back of one of your brushes. Experiment with different sounds and think of each piece of the kit as a separate instrument that can be used as an overdub instrument.

In the following loops I will use some of these concepts and notate them for you. When you are making your own loops, experiment with different sounds.

How to Use the Loops

The loops on the CD will be indexed in each chapter as follows:

The *Full Mix* (FM) is what I call a *performance loop.* This is a real-time performance of drumset and percussion (or just drumset) ranging in time from thirty-five seconds to two minutes in length. There aren't any digital audio edits on any of these grooves. I played to a click in real time from beginning to end. You can import any of these performances from the audio CD into *Pro Tools, Logic,* or whatever program you're using for audio.

Drag your loop from your audio files bin into your session. The next two steps are *very important!*

Set your tempo, and Make sure you line up the clicks exactly with the down-beats.

Otherwise, the loops will be slightly off in time. The software used to burn the audio CD (*Jam, Toast,* or *iTunes*) slightly offsets the starting time of the clicks/audio. You will really have to expand your audio waveform to see the offset of the clicks in relationship to the down-beats. There is always one quarter-note of silence before the start of each set of clicks. Follow these two rules when importing all of the loops from the CD. You can then cut up, edit, and/or duplicate any of these performance loops. Remember that all the loops are stereo mixes.

Drumset only: This is in the thirty seconds range and has no percussion, just drumset. This is usually a twelve- or sixteen-bar phrase that you can manipulate and edit as well.

Percussion only: The same concept as the drumset, this time using percussion only.

Quick Load (QL): The Quick Load loops A, B, and C are the phrase lengths of the groove, so if the groove is a two-bar phrase, the loop of the QL will be a two-bar phrase. You will hear four clicks before the *Full Mix* (FM), which is loop A. You will then hear a rest on beat one, three more clicks, and loop B (drumset only). Then there will be a rest on beat one, three more clicks, and you will hear loop C (percussion only). (Some Quick Load loops are just the Full Mix loop.) You can load and duplicate any of these for instant loops to play along to or compose with. You can easily edit a four-bar QL and make it a two-bar, or turn a two-bar phrase into a one-bar, seamless loop. Most of these loops will duplicate seamlessly, but some will need editing. Use your ears and experiment. The Quick Loads will also be notated in each chapter. The drumset, percussion, cymbals, sticks, and head combinations will be written as well.

Let's get started.

Creating Professional Drum Loops

Loop 1: Olodum

Listen to the full mix performance loop of the hybrid Olodum groove (CD track 1). You will hear bass drum, snare drum, and hi-hat first, played with *Blasticks* by Regal Tip. The next part is an overdub of two tom-toms played with Regal Tip mallets. Then I overdubbed a 16" floor tom and played it like a *surdo* using a mallet. (The *surdo* is a Brazilian kettle-shaped drum that is the heartbeat of the ensemble.) The shaker sound is a rainstick played like a shaker. The improvised percussion part is on a 10" popcorn snare with the snares turned off and played like a timbale. I used thin timbale sticks by Regal Tip to play this part. You can hear drumset only on CD track 2 and percussion only on CD track 3.

Check out the notation for the drumset and percussion in the quick load loops (CD tracks 4 A, B, and C) below. This will help you if you want to learn to play the groove or program it. The drumset used is a maple Pacific *CX* kit: 22" bass drum; 12", 13", and 16" toms; a 14" bronze snare drum; a 10" popcorn snare; and DW *5000 Series* pedals. Cymbals were *Traditional Series Series* from Paiste: 20" ride, 16" and 18" crashes, and 14" hi-hats. Remo *Ambassador* heads were used on the tom-tom tops and *Diplomats* were used on the bottoms. A Remo *Powerstroke 3* was used as the rear bass drum head and a clear *Ambassador* was used as the front head, with a hole cut in the center and a pillow placed inside the drum. I've included a reference chart to help you navigate from loop to loop in each chapter using the CD.

CD Reference Chart

Chapter	Track Name	Description	Track No.	Tempo	Time
2	Olodum	Full Mix	1	♩=96	1:06.47
2	Olodum	Drumset Only	2	♩=96	33.10
2	Olodum	Percussion Only	3	♩=96	33.10
2	Olodum	Quick Load Full Mix	4a	♩=96	23.10
2	Olodum	Quick Load Drumset Only	4b	♩=96	23.10
2	Olodum	Quick Load Percussion Only	4c	♩=96	23.10

Quick Load Drum & Percussion Notation

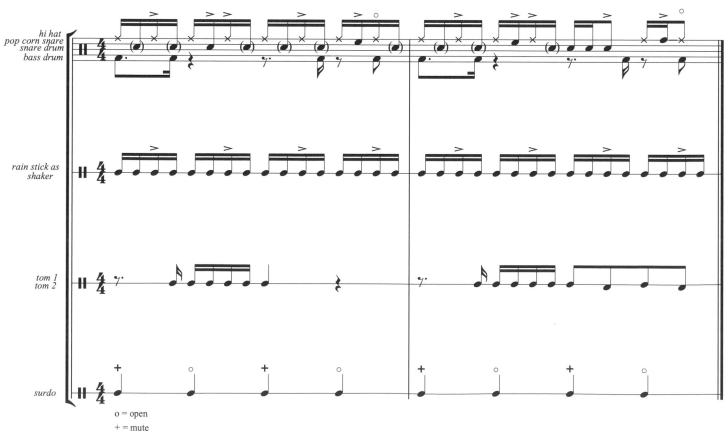

Loop 2: Funk/Hip-Hop

The next full mix performance loop is a programmed groove. The groove is swung slightly and has a funk/hip-hop feel to it. The performance loop starts with a real-time kick, snare, and hi-hat groove recorded with one mono microphone (CD track 5). Over that groove, I overdubbed a 6" Remo *Soundshape* and played brushes on a snare drum with wooden hoops. This groove goes for twelve bars and then the programmed beat comes in and plays out to the end. The brush overdub continues to play through this part as well. I used two different snare samples and two different bass drum samples in the programmed groove along with a hi-hat sample.

The programmed sounds are the Korg *OASYS* card's *Triton* sounds, and I sequenced the groove from a keyboard controller into *Logic*. All the live real-time instruments were recorded into *Pro Tools*. The drumset is a Pacific *LX* 22" bass drum and 14" snare. The snare head is a coated *Ambassador* and the bass drum head is a Powerstroke 3. You can hear drumset only on CD track 6 and percussion only on CD track 7. Look at the notation for the drumset and percussion in the Quick Load loops (CD tracks 8 A, B, and C). This will help you if you want to play or program the groove. Experiment with programming your own beats and then edit them into loops.

The reference chart below will help you navigate from loop-to-loop in each chapter using the CD.

CD Reference Chart

Chapter	Track Name	Description	Track No.	Tempo	Time
2	Funk/Hip-Hop	Full Mix	5	♩=108	:56.09
2	Funk/Hip-Hop	Drumset Only	6	♩=108	:33.67
2	Funk/Hip-Hop	Percussion Only	7	♩=108	:38.05
2	Funk/Hip-Hop	Quick Load Full Mix	8a	♩=108	:20.21
2	Funk/Hip-Hop	Quick Load Drumset Only	8b	♩=108	:20.21
2	Funk/Hip-Hop	Quick Load Percussion Only	8c	♩=108	:20.21

Quick load drum & percussion notation

o = open tone
+ = mute tone

Creating Professional Drum Loops

Loop 3: Tom-Tom groove

The last full mix performance loop in this chapter is a tom-tom groove with a rock feel, a backbeat, a splashy hi-hat overdub in the right hand, and a popcorn snare played with the left hand with the snares off. First I played the tom-tom, snare, and bass drum groove to a click. The toms were played with a Regal Tip mallet in the right hand. The snare was played with the left hand with a thin Regal Tip timbale stick. Listen to CD track 9. Over that groove I overdubbed the hi-hat (14" Paiste *Traditional Series*) and a 10" popcorn snare from Pacific.

The sticks were *Thai Sticks* by Regal Tip.
The drumset is a Pacific CX kit, (22" bass drum, 12" and 14" toms, and a bronze 14" snare drum). The heads were coated *Ambassadors* on the tops and *Diplomats* on the bottoms. The bass drum head was a *Powerstroke 3* on the beater side and a clear *Ambassador* on the front, with a hole cut in the middle and a pillow placed inside for muffling. You can listen to the drumset only (minus the overdub) on CD track 10, and the percussion only (hi-hat and snare overdub) on CD track 11. Look at the notation for the drumset and percussion in the Quick Load loops (CD track 12 A, B, and C). *See the reference chart below.*

CD Reference Chart

Chapter	Track Name	Description	Track No.	Tempo	Time
2	Tom-Tom groove	Full Mix	9	♩=106	:57.08
2	Tom-Tom groove	Drumset Only	10	♩=106	:30.00
2	Tom-Tom groove	Percussion Only	11	♩=106	:30.00
2	Tom-Tom groove	Quick Load Full Mix	12a	♩=106	:20.71
2	Tom-Tom groove	Quick Load Drumset Only	12b	♩=106	:20.71
2	Tom-Tom groove	Quick Load Percussion Only	12c	♩=106	:20.71

Quick load drum & percussion notation

o= open hi hat

Chapter 3 • Hip-Hop Loops

Playing with a Click

Being able to play a groove with a click is very important when you are creating your own drumset and percussion loops. Here are some things to keep in mind when you are recording with a click:

Choose a sound that is easy to play to. I like cowbell with a strong attack and not too much decay. This makes it easier to lock in with. If you use a sound with a long decay sometimes it is hard to differentiate between the front and back end of the sound (for example, with the sidestick). With cowbell I pretend I'm grooving with the percussionist. You have to have the attitude that the cowbell is following you rather than the other way around.

Be careful not to turn the click up too loud in your headphones. It should lay in the track musically (you don't want it ripping your head off with volume). This way you can play in a more relaxed way. When you cancel out the click completely, you're right on it. When you hear it, you are either behind or in front of the click.

Sometimes I like to record a guide-track shaker with the click before I play drumset. Then I can lock in and play with my time-feel (the shaker), and turn the click down in my headphones. In the end, the shaker can be used or not.

When you're tracking the rhythm section all at once, try giving just the drummer the click and have the rest of the rhythm section lock in with the drums. This works great if the drummer has a good time-feel and can lock in with the click comfortably.

Let's move on to the hip-hop loops.

Creating Professional Drum Loops

Loop 4: Hip-Hop 1

Listen to the full mix performance loop (CD track 13). This groove is swung and has a forward loping feeling in the hi-hat. First I played the kick, snare, and hi-hat groove. Then I overdubbed cowbell and tambourine (both by Mountain Rythym). Then I overdubbed a 16" *djembe* (Remo). I used Regal Tip *Groovers* for sticks.

The drumset was a Pacific CX 22" bass drum and 10"

popcorn snare, with DW *5000 Series* pedals and 13" Paiste *Dimensions* hi-hats. The drum heads were Remo *FiberSkyn 3s* on the snare and *Powerstroke 3s* on the bass drum, with a hole in the front head with muffling in the drum.

You can listen to drumset only on CD track 14, and percussion only on CD track 15. Check out the notation for the drumset and percussion for the Quick Load loops (CD tracks 16 A, B, and C). This will assist you if you want to learn to play the groove or program it. *See the reference chart below.*

CD Reference Chart

Chapter	Track Name	Description	Track No.	Tempo	Time
3	Hip-Hop 1	Full Mix	13	♩=115	:49.43
3	Hip-Hop 1	Drumset Only	14	♩=115	:27.59
3	Hip-Hop 1	Percussion Only	15	♩=115	:27.49
3	Hip-Hop 1	Quick Load Full Mix	16 A	♩=115	:31.62
3	Hip-Hop 1	Quick Load Drumset Only	16 B	♩=115	:31.62
3	Hip-Hop 1	Quick Load Percussion Only	16 C	♩=115	:31.62

Quick load drum & percussion notation

Loop 5: Hip-Hop 2

The next loop is a slower, looser hip-hop feel. The full mix performance loop starts out with a 22" bass drum, 14" bronze snare (Pacific), and splashy 14" Paiste *Signature* hi-hats. I used *Groovers* for sticks. In the second section of this full mix I go to a *Noise Works Triple Raw Smash* from Paiste and ride on that cymbal. At that point, the bass drum gets more aggressive (CD track 17). Over that groove, I overdubbed a *CANZ* shaker (Rhythm Tech) and a 10" *djembe* (Remo). The *djembe* has an East Indian feel and gives the time-feel a lift when it comes in. You can hear drumset only on CD track 18, and percussion only on CD track 19.

Look at the notation for the drumset and percussion Quick Load loops (CD tracks 20, A, B, and C). This will assist you if you want to play or program the groove. The reference chart below will help you navigate from loop to loop using the CD.

CD Reference Chart

Chapter	Track Name	Description	Track No.	Tempo	Time
3	Hip-Hop 2	Full Mix	17	♩=88	1:01.28
3	Hip-Hop 2	Drumset Only	18	♩=88	:36.11
3	Hip-Hop 2	Percussion Only	19	♩=88	:32.52
3	Hip-Hop 2	Quick Load Full Mix	20 A	♩=88	:25.18
3	Hip-Hop 2	Quick Load Drumset Only	20 B	♩=88	:25.18
3	Hip-Hop 2	Quick Load Percussion Only	20 C	♩=88	:25.18

Quick load drum & percussion notation

Loop 6: Hip-Hop 3

The next full mix performance loop is a programmed groove. The groove is swung and has a funky hip-hop feel to it. The programmed sounds are the Korg *OASYS Triton* sounds. I used three different bass drums on this groove, combining one tight bass drum sample with a boomy bass drum to create the main kick drum. Then I used a sonic, more open bass drum for some of the boomy downbeats.

I used a high-pitched ringing snare and a noise that I call "weird snare" to play backbeats and ghost notes as well. I used the same effect with a regular hi-hat, playing the

eighth notes panned to the right and a noise hi-hat playing the eighth notes panned to the left. I also used a weird opening hi-hat to accent the end of the two-bar phrase. Check it out (CD track 21). The drums were programmed into *Logic* using a keyboard controller. The groove is quantized using different increments of swing. Next, I overdubbed a 12-inch wooden *djembe cajon* from Mountain Rythym. You can hear drumset only on CD track 22, and percussion only on CD track 23. Check out the notation for the drumset and percussion Quick Loads (CD tracks 24 A, B, and C). This will help you if you want to play or program the groove. *See the reference chart below.*

CD Reference Chart

Chapter	Track Name	Description	Track No.	Tempo	Time
3	Hip-Hop 3 (programmed)	Full Mix	21	♩=86	:53.55
3	Hip-Hop 3 (programmed)	Drumset Only	22	♩=86	:31.30
3	Hip-Hop 3 (programmed)	Percussion Only	23	♩=86	:31.30
3	Hip-Hop 3 (programmed)	Quick Load Full Mix	24A	♩=86	:25.62
3	Hip-Hop 3 (programmed)	Quick Load Drumset Only	24 B	♩=86	:25.62
3	Hip-Hop 3 (programmed)	Quick Load Percussion Only	24 C	♩=86	:25.62

Quick load drum & percussion notation

o = open hi hat
+ = closed hi hat

Loop 7: Hip-Hop 4

The last full mix performance loop is also a programmed loop as well. This loop will only have a full mix and a Quick Load full mix. I programmed the groove into *Logic* from a keyboard controller. The groove has more of a techno hip-hop feel. I used the Korg *OASYS Triton* sounds. The bass drum is very *"TR808"* sounding, with a hi-hat, snare, and sidestick. The second bass drum is very electronic sounding, and there is a sonic delayed sound that moves through the groove. Experiment with programming some of your own beats, and then cut them up and edit them into loops. Listen to CD track 25 for the full performance mix and CD track 26 for the Quick Load loop. Experiment with loading these into *Pro Tools* or the program of your choice and play to the loop or overdub a new part. *The Quick Load full mix is notated after the reference chart below.*

CD Reference Chart

Chapter	Track Name	Description	Track No.	Tempo	Time
3	Hip-Hop 4 (programmed)	Full Mix	25	♩=120	:50.38
3	Hip-Hop 4 (programmed)	Quick Load Full Mix	26	♩=120	:06.38

Quick load drum & percussion notation

Chapter 4 • Funky Loops

Time to get funky. You need to become very aware of "laying for the downbeat" of the groove. Experiment with playing some of your favorite funk and hip-hop beats that have more syncopated bass-drum phrases. Take one of those grooves and just play whole notes on the bass drum. Keep both your left and right hands playing the usual sticking of your groove. Every time the downbeat comes along, be aware of nailing just the whole-note down in the bass drum. Do this for five or ten minutes without changing your kick drum phrase. Really lay for that downbeat in the kick drum and feel that space in between the barlines. When you are comfortable with the whole note, move on to play

half notes on beats one and three. Play that for five or ten minutes, then move on to quarter notes. After you finish with the quarter notes, go back to the whole notes. The next time you get back to the quarter notes, move on to one of the syncopated bass drum phrases that you can really play. Then break down the groove back to the whole note, half note, and quarter note. After doing this for a while you will notice that you feel the down beat of one a little stronger, and you will be able to play all your beats with a more open feel. Let's move on to the first loop of this chapter.

Loop 8: Funk March

Listen to the full mix performance loop (CD track 27). This groove is a slow-funk march. First I played the kick, snare, and hat groove. Then I overdubbed shaker, 16" floor tom (played as a surdo) and lastly, a 4" Remo Soundshape as an improvised part. I used Regal Tip *Jeff Porcaro* sticks. The drumset was a maple Pacific *CX* (22" bass drum and 16" floor tom). A Ludwig Black Beauty snare and DW *5000 Series* pedals were used. The snare heads were *Ambassadors* and the bass drum heads were a *Powerstroke 3* on the beater side and a clear *Ambassador* on the front with a hole cut in the middle with muffling inside. The hi-hats were old Paiste *2002 Sound Edges*. Drumset only is Quick Load (CD track 28). *Check out the notation for the Quick Load loops and reference chart below.*

CD Reference Chart					
Chapter	Track Name	Description	Track No.	Tempo	Time
4	Funk March	Full Mix	27	♩=85	:48.00
4	Funk March	Quick Load Drumset Only	28	♩=85	:14.62

Quick load drum & percussion notation

Loop 9: Drum Cadence

The next loop has a drum cadence feel to it. It's just drumset without any overdubs. I'm playing the march feel on the snare drum, going to the ride cymbal with the right hand, and splashing the hi-hat with the left foot. The bass drum is on beats one and three. Check out CD track 29 (full mix) and CD track 30 (Quick Load). The drumset used was the same as the last loop, with the addition of a 20" Paiste *Traditional Series* ride. *See the reference chart and the notated groove below.*

CD Reference Chart

Chapter	Track Name	Description	Track No.	Tempo	Time
4	Drum Cadence	Full Mix	29	♩=96	:52.38
4	Drum Cadence	Quick Load Drumset Only	30	♩=96	:13.10

Quick load drum & percussion notation

ride cymbal
snare drum
bass drum /
hi hat splash

Loop 10: Funk 1

The next full mix performance loop is a broken sixteenth-note groove (CD track 31). This groove has a straight time-feel and a nice lope to the downbeat. First I played bass drum, snare, and hi-hat to a cowbell click. Then I overdubbed an LP egg shaker, a Mountain Rythym *ashiko* hand drum, and Remo agogo bells. I used thin Regal Tip timbale sticks to play the kick, snare, and hat groove. The bass drum was a Pacific *CX* 22" bass drum with a *Powerstroke 3* head on the beater side and a

clear *Ambassador* with a hole cut in the middle on the front with muffling inside. The snare was a 10" popcorn snare (Pacific) with a *FiberSkyn 3* head. The toms were Pacific *CX* with coated *Ambassador* tops and clears on the bottoms. Listen to the drumset only on CD track 32 and percussion only on CD track 33. Check out the notation for the drumset and percussion for the Quick Load loops (CD track 34, A, B, and C). Be sure to import the Quick Loads into your DAW and edit and duplicate the loops for as many bars as needed to play along with or to use while writing. *See the reference chart below.*

CD Reference Chart

Chapter	Track Name	Description	Track No.	Tempo	Time
4	Funk 1	Full Mix	31	♩=90	:59.46
4	Funk 1	Drumset Only	32	♩=90	:38.50
4	Funk 1	Percussion Only	33	♩=90	:38.21
4	Funk 1	Quick Load Full Mix	34 A	♩=90	:24.50
4	Funk 1	Quick Load Drumset Only	34 B	♩=90	:24.50
4	Funk 1	Quick Load Percussion Only	34 C	♩=90	:24.50

Quick load drum & percussion notation

Loop 11: Funk 2

The next loop is a full performance loop only. Experiment with editing your own Quick Load from the long full mix loop (CD track 35).

I played an old 18" Slingerland bass drum wide open with Remo *FiberSkyn 3* heads on the front and back of the drum with no muffling. The snare is a Pacific 10"

popcorn snare with a *FiberSkyn* head. I used Regal Tip timbale sticks to play the drumset and played the top of the bass drum with my right hand to get that woody clicking sound. I clicked quarter-notes with my left foot on the 14" *Signature Series* hi-hat and played a 17" *Signature Series* crash at the end. I used an LP egg shaker and a Mountain Rythym cowbell. *See the notation and reference chart below.*

Chapter	Track Name	Description	Track No.	Tempo	Time
4	Funk 2	Full Mix	35	♩=104	:34.47

CD Reference Chart

Quick load drum & percussion notation

Loop 12: Funk/Rock 3

The next full mix performance loop has a heavy funk/rock sixteenth-note feel. There is no percussion on this loop. I played kick, snare, and hi-hat to a cowbell click. The bass drum is an old 18" Slingerland with the same head setup as the last loop. The snare is a Pacific popcorn 10" snare with a *FiberSkyn* head. The cymbals are Paiste *2002 Sound Edge* hi-hats and two *Signature Series* crashes (16" and 18"). Check out the full performance mix (CD track 36) and the Quick Load full mix (CD track 37). *See the reference chart and the Quick Load notation below.*

CD Reference Chart

Chapter	Track Name	Description	Track No.	Tempo	Time
4	Funk/Rock 3	Full Mix	36	♩=124	:54.53
4	Funk/Rock 3	Quick Load Full Mix	37	♩=124	:10.13

Quick load drum & percussion notation

Loop 13: Funk 4

The last full mix performance loop in this chapter was influenced by an old James Brown groove. The drumset, cymbal, and head setup is the same as the last loop. Check out the full mix performance on CD track 38 and the Quick Load full mix on CD track 39. The Jackson Five used to play a similar groove as well. There is no percussion on this loop. I did one pass on drumset, playing to a cowbell click. *See the reference chart and notation below.*

CD Reference Chart

Chapter	Track Name	Description	Track No.	Tempo	Time
4	Funk 4	Full Mix	38	♩=133	1:10.63
4	Funk 4	Quick Load Full Mix	39	♩=133	:05.65

Quick load drum & percussion notation

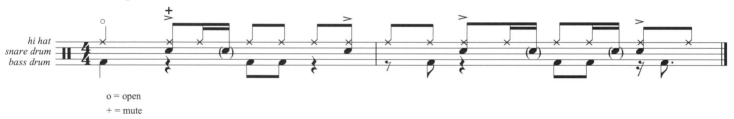

o = open
+ = mute

Chapter 5 • Rock and Blues Loops

Loop 14: Straight-Eighth Rock

The first full mix performance loop in this chapter is a straight-eighth rock groove (CD track 40).

First I played kick, snare, and hi-hat to a quarter note cowbell click. Then I overdubbed cowbell on quarter notes and tambourine playing sixteenth notes. After the eighth-note fill in the middle, the tambourine drops out and I play a splashy hi-hat through to the end. I used Regal Tip *Groover* sticks and a Pacific *CX* drumset with a 22" bass drum, 14"

bronze snare, and 12" and 14" toms. The cymbals were Paiste *Signature Series* 14" hi-hats and 16" and 18" crashes.

The heads were coated *Ambassadors* and the bass drum head was a *Powerstroke 3* on the beater side and an *Ambassador* clear on the front with a hole cut in the middle and muffling. The cowbell and tambourine were from Mountain Rythym. Check out drumset only (CD track 41) and percussion only (CD track 42). The notation for the drumset and percussion Quick Load loops (CD tracks 43 A, B, and C) are on the next page. *See the reference chart below.*

Chapter	Track Name	Description	Track No.	Tempo	Time
5	Straight-Eighth Rock	Full Mix	40	♩=120	1:03.16
5	Straight-Eighth Rock	Drumset Only	41	♩=120	:26.38
5	Straight-Eighth Rock	Percussion Only	42	♩=120	:26.38
5	Straight-Eighth Rock	Quick Load Full Mix	43 A	♩=120	:30.38
5	Straight-Eighth Rock	Quick Load Drumset Only	43 B	♩=120	:30.38
5	Straight-Eighth Rock	Quick Load Percussion Only	43 C	♩=120	:30.38

CD Reference Chart

Quick load drum & percussion notation

o = open

Creating Professional Drum Loops

Loop 15: Rock Shuffle

The next full mix performance loop is a rock shuffle (CD track 44). This groove has a rolling triplet feel, with the ghost notes being played in between the backbeats on two and four. First I played the drumset and then overdubbed the tambourine. The drumset is a Pacific *CX* kit with a 22" bass drum, 12", 14", and 16" toms, and a 14" bronze snare drum. I used Paiste *Traditional Series* cymbals (14" hi-hats, and 16" and 18" crashes). The heads were Remo *Ambassadors*, and I used Regal Tip 8As for sticks. *Check out the notation for the Quick Load full mix (CD track 45) and the reference chart below.*

Chapter	Track Name	Description	Track No.	Tempo	Time
		CD Reference Chart			
5	Rock Shuffle	Full Mix	44	$\quad$=130	00:45.18
5	Rock Shuffle	Quick Load Full Mix	45	$\quad$=130	00:09.52

Quick load drum & percussion notation

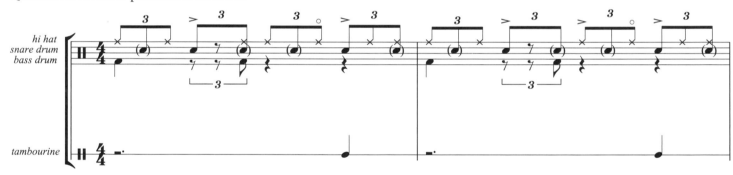

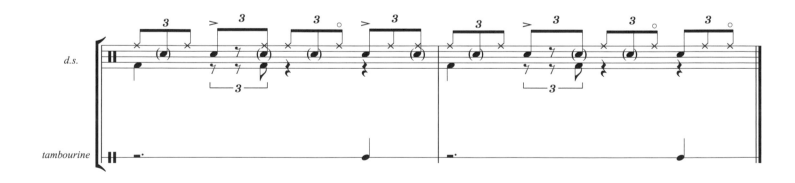

Loop 16: Rock Blues $\frac{12}{8}$

The next full mix performance loop (CD track 46) is a rock/blues $\frac{12}{8}$–feel with a backbeat. The countoff is six eighth notes up front and a fill pickup over three eighth notes to the downbeat. I played the drumset, then overdubbed the frame drum and tambourine (Mountain Rythym). The drumset is a Pacific *CX* kit (22" bass drum, 12", 14", and 16" toms, with a bronze snare drum). I used Paiste *Traditional Series* 16" and 18" crashes and a 20" *Dimensions* ride. The heads were Remo *Ambassadors*, with a *Powerstroke 3* on the bass drum with a hole in the front and muffling. The sticks were Regal Tip 8As. *Check out the notation for the Quick Load full mix (CD track 47) and the reference chart below.*

CD Reference Chart

Chapter	Track Name	Description	Track No.	Tempo	Time
5	Rock Blues $\frac{12}{8}$	Full Mix	46	♩=116	:55.26
5	Rock Blues $\frac{12}{8}$	Quick Load Full Mix	47	♩=116	:09.63

Quick load drum & percussion notation

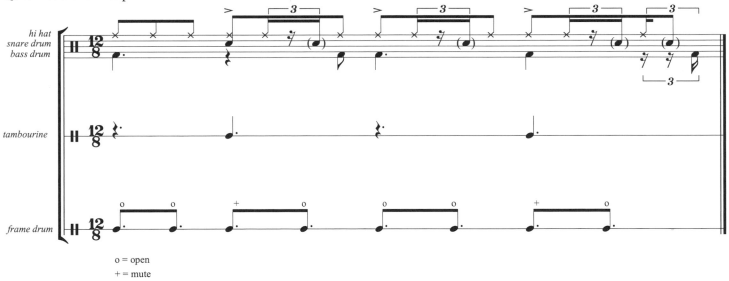

o = open
+ = mute

Loop 17: Slow Blues ¹²⁄₈

The last full mix performance loop in this chapter is a slow blues ¹²⁄₈–feel with a backbeat (CD track 48). The tempo is a little quicker than the last ¹²⁄₈–feel and the drumset (and sound) is completely different. This performance loop is drumset only without any percussion or overdubs.

The drumset is an old 18" Slingerland maple bass drum with *FiberSkyn* heads on the front and back and no muffling inside the drum. The snare is a Pacific 10" popcorn snare, also with a *FiberSkyn* head. I used Regal Tip timbale sticks to play this groove. The cymbals used are Paiste *Traditionals* (20" ride, 16" and 18" crashes, and 14" hi-hats). *Check out the notation for the Quick Load full mix (CD track 49) and the reference chart below.*

(CD Reference Chart)

Chapter	Track Name	Description	Track No.	Tempo	Time
5	Slow Blues ¹²⁄₈	Full Mix	48	♩=126	1:15.18
5	Slow Blues ¹²⁄₈	Quick Load Full Mix	49	♩=126	0:09.04

Quick load drum & percussion notation

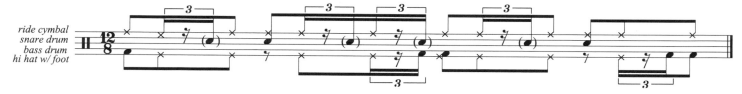

ride cymbal
snare drum
bass drum
hi hat w/ foot

Chapter 6 • Hybrid African Drumset and Percussion Loops

Loop 18: Africa 1

In this chapter I've created three hybrid African drumset and percussion loops. The first full mix performance loop is written out in 𝄴 time with a § feel. The concept for this groove was to start out on a hybrid drumset and create an open §-feeling groove and then overdub other hand drum tones, chants, bells, and whistles. The tones are very melodic in this loop and in those to come (CD track 50).

First I played the drumset. The bass drum has a nice, wide open tone to it. It is an old Slingerland 18" bass drum with *FiberSkyn 3* heads on both sides, wide open with no muffling. The snare is a Pacific 10" popcorn snare with a *FiberSkyn 3* head as well. The toms are *Pacific LX*

maple 10", 12", and 16" toms with *FiberSkyn 3* heads.

I used Paiste *Traditionals* (17" thin crash, 16" fast crash, and 14" medium hi-hats), a 20" *Dimensions* dry ride, and the funky trashy cymbal is a *Noiseworks Triple Raw Smash*. The second snare drum is an *ashiko* 12" from Mountain Rythym. I used *Thai Sticks* (Regal Tip) to play this groove and played to a quarter-note cowbell click. I then overdubbed a rainstick played as a shaker, agogo bells, Remo frame drum, Mountain Rythym *bongo cajons* (improvisation), and a vocal chant track and wooden whistle improvisation. Check out CD track 51 (drumset only) and CD track 52 (percussion only). Check out the Quick Load notation (CD tracks 53 A, B, and C). *See the reference chart below.*

CD Reference Chart					
Chapter	Track Name	Description	Track No.	Tempo	Time
6	Africa 1	Full Mix	50	♩=64	1:54.29
6	Africa 1	Drumset Only	51	♩=64	:31.26
6	Africa 1	Percussion Only	52	♩=64	:31.66
6	Africa 1	Quick Load Full Mix	53 A	♩=64	:34.52
6	Africa 1	Quick Load Drumset Only	53 B	♩=64	:34.52
6	Africa 1	Quick Load Percussion Only	53 C	♩=64	:34.52

Quick load drum & percussion notation

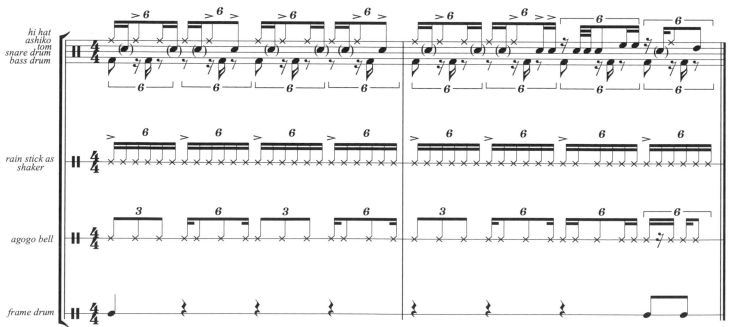

Loop 19: Africa 2

The next full mix performance loop (CD track 54) is in ⁴⁄₄ time with a ⁶⁄₈-feel like the last loop, except the tempo is slower and the drumset groove is a ⁶⁄₈-rock feel with a backbeat.

The drumset used was the same as the last loop. First I played drumset, using thin timbale sticks from Regal Tip. Towards the end of the performance loop, I switched to a

Paiste *Noiseworks Triple Raw Smash* ride cymbal. Then I overdubbed maracas (Mountain Rythym) played as a shaker, a three tom-tom part (12", 14", and 16") played with mallets (Regal Tip), agogo bells (Remo), and a 12" *ashiko* (Mountain Rythym) played with timbale sticks as an improvised part. The cymbal setup was the same as the last loop *(Africa 1)*. Check out drumset only (CD track 55) and percussion only (CD track 56). Check the Quick Load notation (CD tracks 57 A, B, and C). *See the reference chart below.*

CD Reference Chart

Chapter	Track Name	Description	Track No.	Tempo	Time
6	Africa 2	Full Mix	54	♩=55	01:54.41
6	Africa 2	Drumset Only	55	♩=55	:36.00
6	Africa 2	Percussion Only	56	♩=55	:36.00
6	Africa 2	Quick Load Full Mix	57 A	♩=55	:40.28
6	Africa 2	Quick Load Drumset Only	57 B	♩=55	:40.28
6	Africa 2	Quick Load Percussion Only	57 C	♩=55	:40.28

Quick load drum & percussion notation

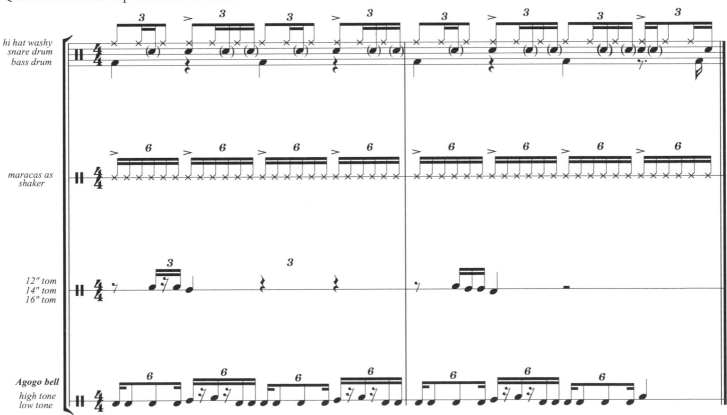

Creating Professional Drum Loops

Loop 20: Africa 3

The last full mix performance loop in this chapter is a $\frac{4}{4}$ African hybrid groove with a hip-hop feel. The drumset is the same as the last two loops. On this groove I played with a thin timbale stick in my right hand and a Regal Tip 8A in my left hand. The hip-hop groove I played is very open in the bass drum and leaves a lot of space for the other instruments (CD track 58). I then overdubbed rainstick as a shaker, a three tom-tom (12", 14", and 16") melodic part with mallets (Regal Tip), a bongo

(Mountain Rythym) part, agogo bells, and a 6" Remo *Soundshape* to play the improvisation part.

All the parts are very simple, but when combined, they create a nice melodic ensemble. Try to combine as many different instruments as possible to create the musical colors that express the style and mood that you are going for in the loops that you create. Check out drumset only (CD track 59) and percussion only (CD track 60). The Quick Load notations are on the next page (CD tracks 61 A, B, and C). *See the reference chart below.*

CD Reference Chart

Chapter	Track Name	Description	Track No.	Tempo	Time
6	Africa 3	Full Mix	58	♩=104	01:36.26
6	Africa 3	Drumset Only	59	♩=104	00:31.55
6	Africa 3	Percussion Only	60	♩=104	00:31.55
6	Africa 3	Quick Load Full Mix	61 A	♩=104	00:35.15
6	Africa 3	Quick Load Drumset Only	61 B	♩=104	00:35.15
6	Africa 3	Quick Load Percussion Only	61 C	♩=104	00:35.15

Quick load drum & percussion notation

Chapter 7 • Samba and Olodum Funk/Rock Loops

Loop 21: Samba 1

In this chapter, the loops will be based on samba, samba march, samba in ⅞, and two hybrid Olodum grooves (funk Olodum and rock Olodum). The first full mix performance loop is a Brazilian samba feel (CD track 62). Samba is usually written in cut time (2/2). The samba has a strong two-feel with an accent on beat two. This is usually played on the *surdo* drum. You can substitute a large floor tom for the *surdo* while playing the drumset, demonstrated on the second loop in this chapter, called *samba march*.

First, I played drumset to a quarter-note cowbell click. The bass drum is an old 20" DW with a *Powerstroke 3* head on the beater side and a clear *Ambassador* on the

front with a hole cut in the middle with muffling.

The drum is set up to have a fat, dead sound. The snare is an old Ludwig *Black Beauty* with a Remo *Ambassador* coated head. The toms are Pacific LX maples with *FiberSkyn 3* heads (tops and bottoms). The second snare is a 10" popcorn snare (Pacific) with a *FiberSkyn 3* head. The cymbals are Paiste *Traditional* 14" medium hats, and 16" and 18" medium thin crashes. Then I overdubbed an LP egg shaker, a 22" *surdo* and agogo bells (both Remo). The drumsticks were Regal Tip *Thai Sticks*. Check CD track 63 (drumset only) and CD track 64 (percussion only). Check the Quick Load notation (CD track 65 A, B, and C). *See the reference chart below.*

Chapter	Track Name	Description	Track No.	Tempo	Time
7	Samba 1	Full Mix	62	♩=104	01:39.61
7	Samba 1	Drumset Only	63	♩=104	0:32.67
7	Samba 1	Percussion Only	64	♩=104	0:32.67
7	Samba 1	Quick Load Full Mix	65 A	♩=104	0:21.26
7	Samba 1	Quick Load Drumset Only	65 B	♩=104	0:21.26
7	Samba 1	Quick Load Percussion Only	65 C	♩=104	0:21.26

CD Reference Chart

Quick load drum & percussion notation

o = open
+ = mute

Creating Professional Drum Loops

Loop 22: Samba March

The next full mix performance loop is a samba march. The groove has a strong two-feel on the 16" floor tom. The floor tom is played like a *surdo* part, and the march is in the snare (CD track 66). The bass drum is the traditional samba bass-drum phrase. The drumset used was the same as the last loop (see page 35), except the floor tom is a 16" instead of a 14", and the head is a coated Remo *Ambassador* on top with a *Diplomat* clear on the bottom. The drum rings out a lot and really helps with the overall feel of the groove. The second snare is an *ashiko* hand drum (Mountain Rythym). I play with *Blasticks* (Regal Tip) to a cowbell click and then overdubbed rainstick as a shaker and a 12" *tubano* hand drum (Remo). The hi-hats were Paiste 14" medium *Traditionals* and the crash was a *Noiseworks Triple Raw Smash*. Check out drumset only (CD track 67) and percussion only (CD track 68). Check the Quick Load notation. (CD track 69 A, B, and C). *See the reference chart below.*

CD Reference Chart					
Chapter	Track Name	Description	Track No.	Tempo	Time
7	Samba March	Full Mix	66	♩=84	1:40.54
7	Samba March	Drumset Only	67	♩=84	0:29.22
7	Samba March	Percussion Only	68	♩=84	0:26.23
7	Samba March	Quick Load Full Mix	69 A	♩=84	0:26.23
7	Samba March	Quick Load Drumset Only	69 B	♩=84	0:26.23
7	Samba March	Quick Load Percussion Only	69 C	♩=84	0:26.23

Quick load drum & percussion notation

Loop 23: Samba in ⅞

The next full mix performance loop is a samba in ⅞.

The seven is subdivided: (♩ ♩ ♩.). I will show you a breakdown of some of the rhythms used. This will help you to get your body to feel the ⅞ pulse.

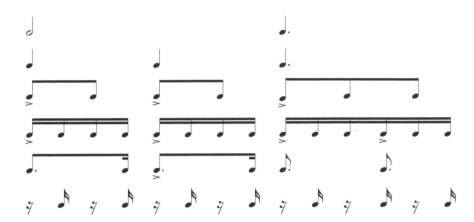

In the drumset groove, I accented the downbeat of the second group of two and the second dotted-eighth note in the phrase. This gave me the feeling of "two" in "seven" (CD track 70).

First, I played drumset to a cowbell click of two quarter notes and a dotted quarter note (♩ ♩ ♩.). The drumset was the same as the last loop (see page 36). I played with

Regal Tip *Jeff Porcaro* sticks, and used a 10" tom (not the 12") with the same head setup as the last loop. Then I overdubbed a Rhythm Tech *CANZ* shaker, a cowbell, and a 12" *djembe cajon* (both from Mountain Rythym), and a talking drum improvised part (Remo). I used the same cymbal setup as the last loop. Check out drumset only (CD track 71) and percussion only (CD track 72). *See the reference chart below.*

CD Reference Chart

Chapter	Track Name	Description	Track No.	Tempo	Time
7	Samba ⅞	Full Mix	70	♩=102	01:37.27
7	Samba ⅞	Drumset only	71	♩=102	0:23.18
7	Samba ⅞	Percussion Only	72	♩=102	0:27.27
7	Samba ⅞	Quick Load Full Mix	73 A	♩=102	0:19.09
7	Samba ⅞	Quick Load Drumset Only	73 B	♩=102	0:19.09
7	Samba ⅞	Quick Load Percussion Only	73 C	♩=102	0:19.09

Quick load drum & percussion notation

Loop 24: Funk Olodum

The next full mix performance loop is a funk Olodum hybrid groove. I played this groove without a click and that's why the tempo is ♩ = 91.92. When I went back to put on a click, that's where the quarter note laid with the groove, so when you import this loop, make sure your tempo is set correctly on CD track 74. I played the drumset first. The set is a 22" DW bass drum, a 14" DW *Edge* snare, and 13" Paiste *Dimensions* hi-hats. The snare is detuned and wide open and has a funky ring to it, which I like. Then I overdubbed an LP egg shaker, a second shaker (Rhythm Tech) used as a one-shot shaker, a Remo *Klong Yaw* hand drum, and a 16" Pacific floor tom played a *surdo*. The heads were Remo *Ambassadors*. Check the Quick Load notation for the full mix Quick Load (CD track 75). *See the reference chart is below.*

CD Reference Chart

Chapter	Track Name	Description	Track No.	Tempo	Time
7	Funk Olodum	Full Mix	74	♩=91.92	0:44.69
7	Funk Olodum	Quick Load Full Mix	75	♩=91.92	0:08.37

Quick load drum & percussion notation

o = open
+ = mute

Loop 25: Rock Olodum

The last full mix performance loop in this chapter is a
rock Olodum hybrid groove. I played kick, snare, and hat
to a quarter-note cowbell click. The drumset was an old
Slingerland 18" bass drum with *FiberSkyn 3* heads on the
front and back, wide open with no muffling. The snare
is a 10" popcorn snare (Pacific) with a *FiberSkyn 3* head,
and the hi-hats are the original Paiste *2002 Sound Edges*
(CD track 76). Then I overdubbed a shaker (Rhythm
Tech) and a tambourine (Mountain Rythym). Check the
notation for the Quick Load full mix (CD track 77).
See the reference chart is below.

CD Reference Chart					
Chapter	Track Name	Description	Track No.	Tempo	Time
7	Rock Olodum	Full Mix	76	♩=104	01:12.09
7	Rock Olodum	Quick Load Full Mix	77	♩=104	00:07.38

Quick load drum & percussion notation

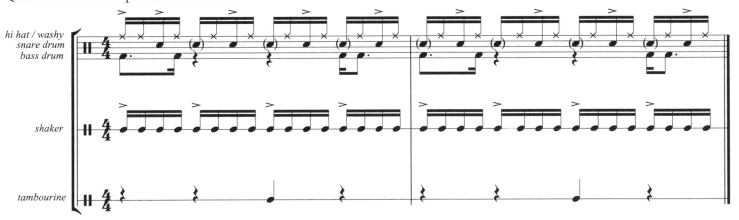

Chapter 8 • Rock Loops & Guest Loops

Loop 26: Funk 5 (Curt Bisquera)

In this last chapter, all the loops will be full mix performance loops and full mix quick loads only. I will also introduce a few special guest drum loops as well.

The first guest loop (CD track 78) is by drummer Curt Bisquera. This is a nice, funky groove with a backbeat. Curt played drumset first to a quarter-note cowbell click. The drumset was a Pacific *CX* maple 22" bass drum, 12", 14", and 16" toms, a bronze 14" snare, and a 10" popcorn snare. The heads were all coated Remo *Ambassadors*, except on the bass drum, which had a Remo *Powerstroke*

3 on the beater side and a clear *Ambassador* on the front, with a hole cut in the middle with muffling.

The hi-hats were Paiste *2002 Sound Edges*, and the cymbals were 16" and 18" Signatures. Curt used Regal Tip *Groover* sticks. He overdubbed a tambourine (Mountain Rythm), and about halfway through, he overdubbed a counter rhythm against his original groove on hi-hat and popcorn snare. I processed that groove with a Tech 21 *SansAmp* plug-in to make it sound electronic. You will hear this groove come in and out. I then overdubbed a 16" floor tom and played a *surdo* part. *The notation for the Quick Load full mix (CD track 79) and the reference chart are below.*

Chapter	Track Name	Description	Track No.	Tempo	Time
8	Funk 5 (Curt Bisquera)	Full Mix	78	♩=100	01:05.30
8	Funk 5 (Curt Bisquera)	Quick Load Full Mix	79	♩=100	00:07.60

CD Reference Chart

Quick load drum & percussion notation

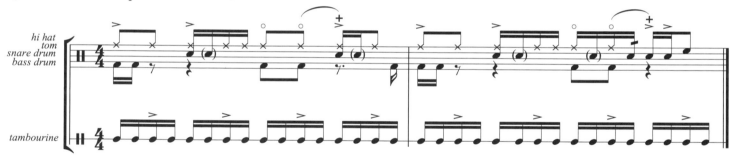

Loop 27: Funk Swing (Joe Porcaro)

The next guest drum loop is by drummer/percussionist Joe Porcaro. This groove (CD track 80) has a nice, funky swing to it. Joe played drumset first to a quarter-note cowbell click. Joe plays left-handed, and the drumset was a Pearl 20" maple bass drum with a *Powerstroke 3* head on the beater side and a clear *Ambassador* on the front with a small hole and very little muffling. The bass drum had a nice open tonal ring to it. The toms were 12" and 16" Pacific *LX*

maples with Remo *Ambassador* heads (tops and bottoms).

The snare was an old Ludwig *Black Beauty* with an *Ambassador* coated head. He used Paiste *2002 Sound Edge* hi-hats, a 20" medium *Traditional* ride, and 16" and 18" Signature Series crashes. Joe used *Joe Porcaro Diamond Tip 5A* sticks. He overdubbed cowbell with a mallet, and a Mountain Rythym tambourine. *See the notation for the Quick Load full mix and the reference chart below.*

CD Reference Chart					
Chapter	Track Name	Description	Track No.	Tempo	Time
8	Funk Swing (Joe Porcaro)	Full Mix	80	♩=100	0:49.15
8	Funk Swing (Joe Porcaro)	Quick LoadFull Mix	81	♩=100	0:07.60

Quick load drum & percussion notation

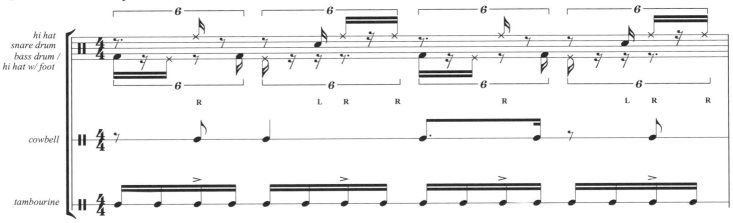

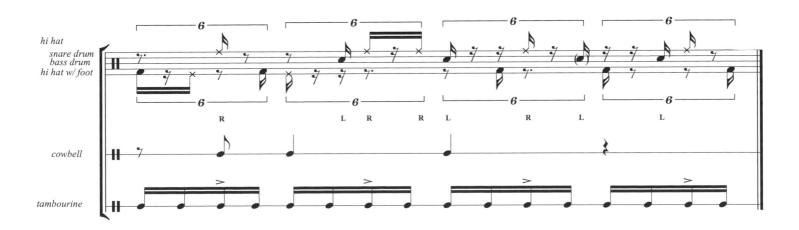

Creating Professional Drum Loops

Loop 28: Rock 1 (Joey C. Cataldo)

The next guest loop is by drummer Joey C. Cataldo (CD track 82). Joey played drumset only with no overdubs on this loop. The groove is a straight-eighth rock groove recorded in a garage. The drums ring out a lot and have a nice live sound to them. The drumset and cymbal setup are the same as the funk Olodum drumset (see page 38). He played to a quarter-note cowbell click at ♩=79. This is a nice open rock groove with a lot of ring and room sound. He used Regal Tip *Groover* sticks. *See the notation for the Quick Load full mix (CD track 83) and the reference chart below.*

CD Reference Chart

Chapter	Track Name	Description	Track No.	Tempo	Time
8	Rock 1(Joey C. Cataldo)	Full Mix	82	♩=79	01:08.56
8	Rock 1(Joey C. Cataldo)	QuickLoad Full Mix	83	♩=79	00:09.66

Quick load drum & percussion notation

Loop 29: Hip-Hop 5

The next full mix performance loop is a hip-hop feel with
a strong downbeat (CD track 84). This is a drumset only
loop with no percussion overdubs. I played kick, snare,
and hi-hat to a cowbell click. The bass drum is an old
Slingerland 18" maple shell with Remo *FiberSkyn 3* heads
on the front and back with no muffling inside the drum.
The bass drum has almost a Roland *TR808* sound. The
snare is a Pacific 10" popcorn snare with a *FiberSkyn 3*
head. The hi-hats are Paiste *2002 Sound Edges*. I used
Regal Tip 8A sticks. *See the notation for the Quick Load
full mix (CD track 85) and the reference chart below.*

CD Reference Chart

Chapter	Track Name	Description	Track No.	Tempo	Time
8	Hip-Hop 5	Full Mix	84	♩=126	01:10.72
8	Hip-Hop 5	Quick Load Full Mix	85	♩=126	0:10.00

Quick load drum & percussion notation

Loop 30: Straight-Eighth Rock 2

The next full mix performance loop is a medium slow,
big straight-eighth-rock groove. This is a very ambient
sounding loop with big room reverb on the snare drum.
This loop (CD track 86) is a drumset only loop with no
percussion overdubs. I played kick, snare, and hi-hat to a
cowbell click. The bass drum is a 22" Pacific *LX* maple
with a small hole cut in the bottom of the front head
with muffling. The hi-hats were Paiste *2002 Sound Edges*.
The snare was a 14" Pacific with a coated Remo
Ambassador head. I used Regal Tip *Jeff Porcaro* sticks.
See the notation for the Quick Load full mix
(CD track 89) and the reference chart below.

CD Reference Chart

Chapter	Track Name	Description	Track No.	Tempo	Time
8	Straight-Eighth Rock 2	Full Mix	86	♩=87	00:53.08
8	Straight-Eighth Rock 2	Quick Load Full Mix	87	♩=87	00:08.73

Quick load drum & percussion notation

Loop 31: Sixteenth-Note Rock (Industrial)

The next full mix performance loop (CD track 88) is a sixteenth-note rock groove with big toms. The kick drum is on one and three and really anchors the groove while the toms are in melodic motion and the snare plays the backbeat. I played the drumset first to a quarter-note cowbell click. The drumset was a Pacific *CX* maple kit with a 22" bass drum, 12", 14", and 16" toms, and a bronze 14" snare. The heads were all Remo coated *Ambassadors* on the tops and *Diplomats* on the bottoms. The bass drum head was a Remo *Powerstroke 3* on the beater side and a clear *Ambassador* on the front with a hole cut in the center with muffling. The hi-hats were Paiste *2002 Sound Edges*. I used Regal Tip *Groover* sticks. Then I overdubbed Regal Tip brushes on a 15" wooden Pacific snare drum with wood hoops to give the groove a train effect. *See the notation for the Quick Load loop (CD track 89) and the reference chart below.*

CD Reference Chart

Chapter	Track Name	Description	Track No.	Tempo	Time
8	Sixteenth-Note Rock with Toms	Full Mix	88	♩=96	01:05.47
8	Sixteenth-Note Rock with Toms	Quick Load Full Mix	89	♩=96	0:08.10

Quick load drum & percussion notation

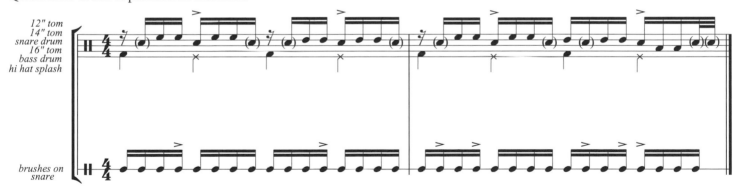

Creating Professional Drum Loops

Loop 32: Rock §

The next full mix performance loop is a §-rock groove
(CD track 90). This is a drumset only loop. I played
drumset to a dotted-quarter-note click. The drumset is
the same as the last loop. I used Paiste *Signature Series*
crash cymbals, *2002 Sound Edge* hi-hats, and Regal Tip
Jeff Porcaro sticks. *See the notation for the Quick Load
loop (CD track 91) and the reference chart below.*

CD Reference Chart

Chapter	Track Name	Description	Track No.	Tempo	Time
8	Rock §	Full Mix	90	♩·=94	01:27.34
8	Rock §	Quick Load Full Mix	91	♩·=94	0:06.29

Quick load drum & percussion notation

o= open hi hat

Loop 33: Funk Rock ⅞

The last full mix performance loop (CD track 92) is a ⅞ funk-rock groove. The subdivision for the seven is the same subdivision I used in the ⅞ samba (♩ ♩ ♩.); *i.e.*, two-plus-two-plus-three. Below is a rhythm chart to help you.

First I played drumset to a (♩ ♩ ♩.) click. The drumset and cymbal setup is the same as the last loop. I used Regal Tip *Groovers*, and then I overdubbed Regal Tip *Thai Sticks*—my drum tech held one stick horizontally in two hands while I hit that stick with two sticks. *See the Quick Load notation and the reference chart below (CD track 93).*

CD Reference Chart

Chapter	Track Name	Description	Track No.	Tempo	Time
8	Funk Rock ⅞	Full Mix	92	♩=120	01:13.38
8	Funk Rock ⅞	Quick Load Full Mix	93	♩=120	00:05.57

Quick load drum & percussion notation

In closing I would like to say keep groovin' and experimenting while creating your drum and percussion loops. Try new drumset, cymbal, and percussion setups and combinations. It's a computer world, but remember to interact with people to make music. There is nothing like capturing a real-time performance.

You can correspond with Ed at, bpmrecords@earthlink.net or visit his websites at www.worldbeatrhythms.com or www.roscettimusic.com

Acknowledgements

Thanks for Your Support:
Scott Donnell, Garrison and Don Lombardi (Drum Workshop/Pacific)
Rich Mangicaro, Ed Clift and Steve Jacobs (Paiste)
Carol Calato and Nick Mason (Regal Tip)
Matt Connors, Michelle Jacoby, Chris Hart, Layne Davy & Brock Kaericher (Remo)
Ryan Goldin (Mountain Rythym)
Ryan Smith (Shure, Inc.)
Yoav & Jeff Stern (Puresound)
Chandra Lynn (DigiDesign)
Rick Naqvi (Presonus)
Michael Marans (Event Electronics)
Jimmy Carnelli and Tom Henry (Drum Tech)

Ed Roscetti uses the following equipment and software:
Pacific LX/CX Series Drumset (Drum Workshop/Pacific) www.pacificdrums.com
Paiste Cymbals & Gongs (Paiste) www.paiste.com,
Remo Drum Heads and World Percussion (Remo) www.remo.com
Shakers (Canz) (Rhythm Tech) www.rhythmtech.com
Sticks, Brushes and Mallets (Regal Tip) www.regaltip.com
KSM 32s, 44s, KSM 27s and Beta Series Microphones (Shure, Inc.) www.shure.com
20/20 Biamplified Studio Monitors & 5.1 Surround (Event Electronics) www.event1.com
Protools LE (001) & HD (DigiDesign) www.digidesign.com
Unitor II MK and Logic Platinum, EXS-24 & EVP-88 software (Emagic/Apple)
Digimax Mic Pre (PreSonus) www.presonus.com

Roscetti has worked or collaborated with: Quincy Jones, Herbie Hancock, Joe Sample, the Crusaders, Benny Golson, Robben Ford, Jeff Baxter, Tommy Tedesco, Joe Porcaro and Jeff Porcaro, and many others.

Ed endorses the following companies: Drum Workshop/Pacific, Paiste, Remo, Regal Tip, Mountain Rythym, Shure Inc., Event Electronics, Emagic, Digidesign, PreSonus, and Puresound.

Special thanks to:
Claudia Dunn, John Hartmann, Cory Flanigan, Joe Porcaro, Curt Bisquera, Joe Cataldo, Maria Martinez, Theresa and Michael Robertson, Louie Marino, Groovetoons, Ed Lozano, and everyone at Music Sales Corporation.

CD Produced by Ed Roscetti, groovetoons (ASCAP) © 2004 All Rights Reserved.

Drum and percussion loops performed, programmed and arranged by: Ed Roscetti

Guest Loops by: Joe Porcaro, Curt Bisquera, and Joe Cataldo

Recorded at Groovetoons, Studio City, California, by John Hartmann.

Mixed and Edited at Groovetoons, Studio City, California, by John Hartmann and Ed Roscetti

DAW/Studio Tech: John Hartmann
CD Mastering: John Hartmann
Drum Tech/Cartage: Cory Flanigan
Loop Transcriptions: Cory Flanigan

Dedication:
This book is dedicated to my family, Claudia, Linda, Armeto and Ann.